Siddhant Kale
Praveen Mali
Ashutosh Mokate

The Effect of MoS2 on Friction & Wear Behavior of PTFE Composites

Anchor Academic
Publishing

Kale, Siddhant, Mali, Praveen, Mokate, Ashutosh: The Effect of MoS2 on Friction &
Wear Behavior of PTFE Composites, Hamburg, Anchor Academic Publishing 2016

Buch-ISBN: 978-3-96067-025-4
PDF-eBook-ISBN: 978-3-96067-525-9
Druck/Herstellung: Anchor Academic Publishing, Hamburg, 2016

Bibliografische Information der Deutschen Nationalbibliothek:
Die Deutsche Nationalbibliothek verzeichnet diese Publikation in der Deutschen
Nationalbibliografie; detaillierte bibliografische Daten sind im Internet über
http://dnb.d-nb.de abrufbar.

Bibliographical Information of the German National Library:
The German National Library lists this publication in the German National Bibliography.
Detailed bibliographic data can be found at: http://dnb.d-nb.de

© Anchor Academic Publishing, Imprint der Diplomica Verlag GmbH
Hermannstal 119k, 22119 Hamburg
http://www.diplomica-verlag.de, Hamburg 2016
Printed in Germany

TABLE OF CONTENTS

1. INTRODUCTION

Tribology is the science of rubbing surfaces in relative motion. It is the study of the friction, wear and lubrication of engineering surfaces with a view of understanding surface interactions in detail and then prescribing improvements in given applications. One of the important objectives in tribology is the regulation of the magnitude of frictional force according to whether we require a minimum or a maximum. This objective can be realized only after a fundamental understanding of the frictional process for all conditions like load, sliding velocity, lubrication, surface finish,temperature and material properties. [1]

For over sixty years, our world and the quality of its inhabitant's lives have been improved by a resin known as polytetrafluoroethylene or PTFE. It is discovered in 1938 by a DuPont chemist, Mr. Roy J. Plunkett. Upon examination, DuPont learned that PTFE provided a combination of friction, temperature, chemical, mechanicaland electrical resisting properties. PTFE ([C2F4]n) is recorded in The Guinness Book of World Records for the lowest coefficient of static and dynamic friction as 0.02 - equivalent to wet ice on wet ice.[1]

PTFE is a kind of self-lubricating material having super low coefficient of friction, outstanding corrosion resistance, chemical inertness and wide service temperature range. [2]PTFE is a frequently used solid lubricant both as filler and matrix.[3] PTFE is currently finding increasing utility in high performance mechanical seals due to its unique properties like high chemical resistivity, low coefficient of friction and high temperature stability. However, its application has been greatly limited due to its poor mechanical properties, high linear expansion coefficient, bad thermal conductivity and poor wear and abrasion resistance. [3, 4]

The wear resistance of PTFE can be significantly improved by addition of suitable filler materials. Besides the type, the shape and size of the materials added also influence the tribological properties. In the past, research in this area has been confined to the PTFE filled with conventional filler materials like glass fibers, graphite, carbon fibers, etc. However, with the growing demand for utilizing PTFE in a variety of applications, significant effort is needed towards developing the novel composite materials by adding one or more non-conventional filler materials possessing the potential of increasing the wear resistance. It is established that PTFE exhibits significantly low coefficient of friction when sliding against steels. The low coefficient of friction results from the ability of its extended chain linear molecules, $-(CF_2-CF_2)$ $n-$, to form low shear strength films upon its surface and mating counter-faces during sliding. [1]

PTFE is extensively used for a wide variety of structural applications as in aerospace, automotive, earth moving, medical, electrical, electronics, computer and chemical industries. On account of its good combination of properties, these are used for producing a number of mechanical components such as gears, cams, wheels, brakes, clutches, bearings, gaskets, seals as well as wires, cables, textile fibers, electronic components, medical implants, surgical instruments etc.

The needs and advantages of accelerated wear testing are discussed, with particular reference to aerospace applications. Examples are given from recent work on plastics based dry-bearing liners to illustrate how accelerated wear tests can provide information relevant to materials selection, identification of the main parameters influencing wear and definition of the relationships between wear, material composition and structure. Prediction of the service life of dry-bearing liners, however, presents problems and full-scale component tests are usually required. [4]

Surface texturing is the combination of the imperfection on the surface of a part, roughness, waviness, lay and flaws make a surface texture. Surface texturing takes place on the disc which consists of the different dimple size in μ and different dimple density. So, compare the readings of same dimple sizes in μ and dimple density and discuss on the result on wear and coefficient of friction. We use EN304 stainless steel disc. On that disc, three dimple tracks are takes place having different diameters and μ sizes (100 μ, 200 μ, 300 μ). On plane surface also takes the reading. Compare the reading on plane surfaces and texturing surfaces and discuss the results on wear and coefficient of friction.

In this work attention is given to investigate the tribological properties of composite materials considering various conditions so as to observe the comparative friction and wear behavior of PTFE composite interfaced with graded fillers under constant loads and sliding velocities by using a pin-on-disc type wear tester at NTP. Experimental work will be carried out considering velocity i.e.0.12 m/skeepingrest of the parameters constant. The test will be carried out for two materials, 85 % PTFE + 15 % Glass Fiber and 80 % PTFE + 15 % GF + 5 % MoS_2 by weight, in dry condition. In this work EN304 stainless steel disc will be used as counterpart surface and tests will be carried out at ambient conditions using a pin-on-disc Tribometer (TR-20LE).The influence of the fillers, on the wear of the PTFE composite under dry sliding conditions against the EN304 stainless steel disc will try to investigate and their sliding wear performance will compared with PTFE + GF material.

2

2. LITERATURE REVIEW

JaydeepKhedkar, IoanNegulescu, Efstathios I. Meletis(2002) "Sliding wear behavior of PTFE composites" They experimented that the tribological behavior of polytetrafluroethylene (PTFE) and PTFE composites with filler materials such as carbon, graphite, E glass fibers, MoS2 and poly-*p*-phenyleneterephthalamide (PPDT) fibers, was studied. The present filler additions found to increase hardness and wear resistance in all composites studied. The highest wear resistance was found for composites containing (i) 18% carbon + 7% graphite, (ii) 20% glass fibers + 5% MoS_2 and (iii) 10% PPDT fibers. Scanning electron microscopy (SEM) was utilized to examine composite microstructures and study modes of failure. Wear testing and SEM analysis showed that three-body abrasion was probably the dominant mode of failure for PTFE + 18% carbon + 7% graphite composite, while fiber pull out and fragmentation caused failure of PTFE + 20% glass fiber + 5% MoS_2 composite. The composite with 10% PPDT fibers caused wear reduction due to the ability of the fibers to remain embedded in the matrix and preferentially support the load. Differential scanning calorimetry (DSC) analysis was also performed to study the relative heat absorbing capacity and thermal stability of the various composites in an effort to correlate these properties to the tribological performance. The results indicated that composites with higher heat absorption capacity exhibited improved wear resistance. The dominant interactive wear mechanisms during sliding of PTFE and its composites are discussed in view of the present findings. From that they concluded that Addition of filler materials such as carbon, graphite, glass fibers and PPDT to PTFE causes an increase in hardness and wear resistance, while the coefficient of friction is slightly affected and remains low. Filler materials in general are effective in impeding large-scale fragmentation of PTFE, thereby reducing the wear rate. The wear process in the composites depends mainly on three factors: thermal stability, thermal conductivity, and the characteristics of the filler materials. IN the presence of a strengthening phase such as glass fibers, MoS_2 particles were found to be very effective in improving the wear properties of the composite. [5]

Dr. G.J.Vikhe, K.B.Kale&J.L.Shindein(2008) **"An Investigation of tribological behavior of MoS₂ on PTFE composites"** they experimented that effect of addition of MoS_2 in PTFE composites (Bronze & Glass Fiber) on tribological properties are studied. In this paper, experimental evaluation of tribological properties is done with help of Pin-on-Disc (TR-20) Tribometer to find the wear rate and coefficient of friction. The tests were carried out in different environments like dry & humid. Also a case study is being done on sealing materials in compressors and they concluded that it is observed from the graphs of wear that in dry condition addition of 5% of MoS_2 toPTFE+15%GF matrix increases wear against both counter surface Grey CI & ChromiumPlate. This is according to Liu et al. that MoS_2 was not very effective for reducing friction andcaused an increase in wear. Also Bijwe et al. proposed that the addition of MoS_2 alone didnot impart a good wear resistance to PTFE, especially during severe conditions of slidingGrey C.I. & Chromium Plate.While addition of 5% MoS_2 in PTFE+60% Bronze wear decreases against both countersurface Grey CI & Chromium Plate. This is due to formation of PTFE bronze composite filmon the counter surface (disc). It is the result of the fact that adhesion force between the firstcomposite wear products (pin) and counter surface (disc) is greater than the cohesion forcebetween first composite wear products and counter surface causing good compositetransfer film reducing wear. The filler particles in the current composite are expected toprovide a blocking action on the slip of the PTFE lamellae and thereby to reduce the wearrate.Frictional force decreases with addition of MoS_2 in PTFE + 15% GF as well as for PTFE +60% Bronze. Also reduction of frictional force is seen more in PTFE + 60% Bronze comparedto PTFE + 15% GF matrix. This may be due to addition of lubricating MoS_2 in the presence ofa strengthening phase has the potential to reduce the friction by the latter by maintaining allow friction film. Wear increases with addition of MoS_2 in PTFE +15% GF in humid environment. Highhumidity enables the rate at which MoS_2 oxidizes to increase. The oxidation productmolybdenum trioxides (MoO_3) possess abrasive properties, and the sulphur acid which forms when this occurs may cause severe corrosive wear. While it remains all the most same forthe PTFE + 60% Bronze matrix. Frictional force increases with addition of MoS_2 in PTFE + 15% GF in humid environment. An increase in the temperature in the friction zone causes partial oxidation of the MoS_2 in the areas of the actual contact surface forming H_2S immediately in large quantities, and thefriction coefficient increases until it reached a maximum value, after which it graduallydropped again to a lower value. Frictional force decreases with addition of PTFE+60%Bronzematrix in humid environment against both counter surfaces.Wear resistance of PTFE +15% GF + MoS_2 shows slightly better results as compared toPTFE+60%Bronze + MoS_2 but, properties of PTFE + 60%Bronze + MoS_2 are more suitable for gas compressors like thermal conductivity, coefficient of linear expansion, compressivestrength & is thus recommended for the piston rings of gas compressors. High humidity enables the rate at which MoS_2 oxidizes to increase, causing corrosive wear.Glass fibers with the presence of a small amount of MoS_2 particulates

4

(5%) in PTFE cause asignificant decrease in the wear resistance.PTFE + 60 % Bronze composite with the presence of a small amount of MoS$_2$particulates (5%) cause a significant increase in the wear resistance and frictional force in both humid &dry condition & is thus recommended for gas compressors. [6]

ArashGolchin, Gregory F Simmons and Sergei B Glavatskih " Break-away friction of PTFE materials in lubricated conditions" experimented that This study investigates the tribological characteristics at the initiation of sliding (break-away friction) of several polytetrafluoroethylene (PTFE) based materials including virgin PTFE (PP), PTFE filled with 25% black glass (PG), PTFE filled with 40% Bronze (PB), PTFE filled with 25% Carbon (PC), andPTFE filled with 20% glass fiberand 5% Molybdenum disulphide (PM), as well as standard white-metal Babbitt (BA) in lubricated sliding contact with a steel counter-face. Experiments were carried out using a reciprocating tribo-meter in the block on plate configuration with the specific goal of determining the friction characteristics at break-away under varying conditions. Apparent contact pressures of 1 to 8 MPa were applied with oil temperature levels of 25° to 85°C. Bronze- and carbon-filled PTFE and virgin PTFE were found to provide generally lower break-away friction and less variation in break-away friction over the course of testing than the other tested materials. Break-away friction tests after an extended stop under loading found bronze- and carbon-filled PTFE and virgin PTFE to be minimally affected by the extended stop whereas Babbitt produced a significant increase in break-away friction in the first cycle after stopping. Break-away friction for the four tested materials after an extended stop returned to pre-stop values after 1 stroke. [7]

H. Unal, A. Mimaroglu, U. Kadıoglu, H. Ekiz (2006) "Sliding friction and wear behavior of polytetrafluoroethylene and its composites under dry conditions"they experimented that and they studied and explored the influence of test speed and load values on the friction and wear behavior of purepolytetrafluoroethylene (PTFE), glass fiber reinforced (GFR) and bronze and carbon (C) filled PTFE polymers. Friction and wearexperiments were run under ambient conditions in a pin-on-disc arrangement. Tests were carried out at sliding speed of 0.32, 0.64,0.96 and 1.28 m/s and under a nominal load of 5, 10, 20 and 30 N. The results showed that, for pure PTFE and its compositesused in this investigated, the friction coefficient decrease with the increase in load. The maximum reductions in wear rate and frictioncoefficient were obtained by reinforced PTFE +17% glass fibers. The wear rate for pure PTFE was in the order of 10 7 mm^2/N, whilethe wear rate values for PTFE composites were in the order of 10 8 and 10 9 mm^2/N. Adding glass fiber, bronze and carbon fillers toPTFE were found effective in reducing the wear rate of the PTFE composite. In addition, for the range of load and speeds used inthis investigation, the wear rate showed very little sensitivity to test speed and large sensitivity to the applied load, particularly athigh load values. And they concluded that Wear studies against AISI 440C stainless disccounter face under various loads and sliding speeds,materials used in this study were ranked as followsfor their wear performance. PTFE+ 17% GFR>PTFE+ 25% bronze>PTFE + 35% C>pure PTFE.PTFE + 17% GFR exhibited best wear performance (K0 in the order of 10_8 mm^2/N) and can be consideredas a very good tribo-material between materials used in this study. The friction coefficient of pure PTFE and its compositesdecreases when applied load increases. Pure PTFE is characterized by high wear because ofits small mechanical properties. Therefore, the reinforcementPTFE with glass fibersimproves the loadcarrying capability that lowers the wear rate of thePTFE.For the specific range of load and speed explored inthis study, the load has stronger effect on the wear behavior of PTFE and its composites than the sliding velocity. [8]

Seong Su Kim, HakGu Lee, &Dai Gil Lee (2007)"Thetribological behavior of polymer coated carbon compositesunder dry and water lubricating conditions" were performed wear experiments on pin-on-disk on carbon epoxy composite specimens with many small surface grooves with respect to epoxy (EP) and polyethylene (PE) surface coating materials with and without self-lubricating powders (MoS_2 and PTFE). From the experiments they have showed that, the friction coefficient of the grooved specimen for the case of PE-based coating decreased 5% compared to that of uncoated specimen because of the low hardness and friction coefficient of the PE-based coating. The friction coefficients of the PE + MoS_2 and EP + MoS_2 decreased 9% compared to those with PE + PTFE and EP + PTFE. The PE + MoS_2 coated specimen showed an excellent wear resistance under water lubricating condition.In this work pin on disk wear experiments were performedon carbon epoxy composite specimens with many small surface grooves of 100 µm with respect to epoxy (EP) and polyethylene (PE) surface coating materials with and without self-lubricating powders ($MoS_2$and PTFE). From the experiments, the following results were obtained The friction coefficient of the grooved specimen for the case of PE-based coating decreased 5% compared to that of uncoated specimen because of the low hardness and friction coefficient of the PE-based coating. The friction coefficients of the PE + $MoS_2$and EP + MoS_2 decreased 9% compared to those with PE + PTFE and EP + PTFE. The PE coated and PE + MoS_2coated specimen reduced the wear

6

on the sliding surface due to the embedment of abrasive particles in the coating layer, which prevented fibers from being deboned out of the ridges. The PE + MoS$_2$ coated specimen showed an excellent wear resistance under water lubricating condition, because the mixture of harder MoS$_2$lamellaand soft PE lamellae was less prone to blistering compared to the specimen coated with soft film alone. [9]

Yunxia Wang and Fengyuan Yan (2006) "Tribological properties of transfer films of PTFE-based composites" have carried out the wear test on PTFE-based composites containing 15 vol. % MoS$_2$, graphite, aluminum and bronze powder. Transfer films of pure PTFE and these composites were prepared on the surface of AISI-1045 steel bar using a pin on disc wear tester.Tribological properties of these transfer films were investigated using another tribometer by sliding against GCr15 steel ball in a point-contacting configuration. Morphology of the transfer films and worn surface of the steel ball were observed and analyzed using SEM and optical microscopy. From this study they have showed that, the wear life of the transfer film of PTFE is short because PTFE cannot form durable transfer film on the steel counter face. PTFE is apt to form big flakes and left the contacting region during the friction process. They concluded that The wear life of the transfer film of PTFE is short because PTFE cannot form durable transfer film on the steel counterface. PTFE is apt to form big flakes and left the contacting region during the friction process. The transfer films containing different fillers have different morphologies and structures and hold different load bearing capabilities. Transfer film of the composite could carry out obvious back-transfer to the composite, which effectively reduced wear of the composite. Some inorganic materials, for example, MoS$_2$, graphite, aluminum and bronze power as fillers could effectively prolong the wear life of transfer film of PTFE-based composites. This was mainly achieved by strongly adhering transfer film and smaller wear debris particles or fine fillers stably stay in the roughness valley. Tribological properties of these transfer films are sensitive to load change. Generally, increased load shortened wear life of transfer film. [10]

H. Unal a, U. Sen a, A. Mimarogluhas (2006) "An approach to friction and wear properties of polytetrafluoroethylene composite" and explored the influence of test speed and load values on the friction and wear behavior of pure Polytetrafluoroethylene (PTFE), glass fiber reinforced (GFR) and bronze and carbon (C) filled PTFE polymers. Friction and wear experiments were run under ambient conditions in a pin-on-disc arrangement. Tests were carried out at sliding speed of 0.32 m/s, 0.64 m/s, 0.96 m/s and 1.28 m/s and under a nominal load of 5 N, 10 N, 20 N and 30 N. From this study the have observed that, PTFE + 17% GFR exhibited best wear performance and is a very good tribo-material between materials used in this study. The friction coefficient of pure PTFE and its composites decreases when applied load increases. Pure PTFE is characterized by high wear because of its small mechanical properties. Therefore, the reinforcement PTFE with glass fibers improves the load carrying capability that lowers the wear rate of the PTFE. For the specific range of load and speed explored in this study, the load has stronger effect on the wear behavior of PTFE and its composites than the sliding velocity. [11]

J.K. Lancaster (1982) "Accelerated wear testing as an aid to failure diagnosis and materials selection" wasperformedthe needs and advantages of accelerated wear testing are discussed, with particular reference to aerospace applications. Examples are given from recent work on plastics-based dry-bearing liners to illustrate how accelerated wear tests can provide information relevant to materials selection, identification of the main parameters influencing wear and definition of the relationships between wear, material composition and structure. Prediction of the service life of dry-bearing liners, however, presents problems and full-scale component tests are usually required. [12]

3. BASIC FUNDAMENTALS

3.1 Engineering Materials

The knowledge of materials and their properties is a great significance for a design engineers. Materials are divided into following four types.

1. Metals

2. Ceramics

3. Polymers

4. Composites

3.1.1 Metals

Metals are elements that generally have good electrical and thermal conductivity. Many metals have high strength, high stiffness, and have good ductility. Some metals, such as iron, cobalt and nickel are magnetic. The most important properties of metals include density, fracture toughness, strength and plastic deformation. The atomic bonding of metals also affects their properties. [13]

i) Pure Metals

Pure metals are elements which come from a particular area of the periodic table. Examples of pure metals include copper in electrical wires and aluminum in cooking foil and beverage cans.

ii) Metal Alloys

Metal Alloys contain more than one metallic element. Their properties can be changed by changing the elements present in the alloy. Examples of metal alloys include stainless steel which is an alloy of iron, nickel, and chromium; and gold jewelry which usually contains an alloy of gold and nickel. Many metals and alloys have high densities and are used in applications which require a high mass-to-volume ratio. Some metal alloys, such as those based on Aluminum, have low densities and are used in aerospace applications for fuel economy. Many metal alloys also have high fracture toughness, which means they can withstand impact and are durable. [13]

3.1.2 Ceramics

A ceramic is often broadly defined as any inorganic nonmetallic material. Examples of such materials can be anything from NaCl (table salt) to clay (a complex silicate). Some of the useful properties of ceramics and glasses include high melting temperature, low density, high strength, stiffness, hardness, wear resistance, and corrosion resistance. Many ceramics are good electrical and thermal insulators. Some ceramics have special

9

properties: some ceramics are magnetic materials; some are piezoelectric materials; and a few special ceramics are superconductors at very low temperatures. Ceramics and glasses have one major drawback that they are brittle in nature. [13]

3.1.3 Polymers

A polymer has a repeating structure, usually based on a carbon backbone. The repeating structure results in large chainlike molecules having chemical bonding and synthesized by the polymerization process. Polymers are useful because they are lightweight and corrosion resistant, are easy to process at low temperatures, have good strength to weight ratio and are generally inexpensive. Also they are poor conductors of electricity and heat, which makes them good insulators. Some important characteristics of polymers include their low molecular weight, softening and melting points, crystallinity, and structure. The mechanical properties of polymers generally include low strength and high toughness. Their strength can be improved by reinforced composite structures. [14]

Classification of polymers

According to their mechanical and thermal behavior, polymers are classified as thermoplastics, thermosetting polymers and elastomers.

i) Thermoplastics

Thermoplastics are composed of long chains produced by joining together monomers, typically behave in a plastic ductile manner and may or may not have branches. On heating they become soft and melt to mold into shapes and are easily recycled. Polyamide, polyethylene, PVC, PTFE, acrylic, nylon, PEEK etc. are the examples of thermoplastics.

ii) Thermosetting Polymers

Thermosetting Polymers are composed of long chains (linear or branched) of molecules that strongly cross linked to one another to form three dimensional network structures. They are stronger but brittle than thermoplastics. On heating they do not melt but decompose and hence recycling is difficult. Phenolic, urethanes, amines, polyesters epoxies etc are the examples of thermosetting polymers.

iii) Elastomers

Elastomers are nothing but rubbers and have high elastic deformation (>200%). The polymer chain consists of coil like molecules that can reversibly stretch by applying a force. Natural rubbers, polyisoprene, polybutadiene, butadiene styrene, silicones etc. are the examples of elastomers.

3.1.4 Composites

Composite materials (composites) are engineered materials made from two or more constituent materials with significantly different physical or chemical properties and which remain separate and distinct on a macroscopic level within the finished structure. Composites are widely used because overall properties of the composites are superior to those of the individual components.

There are two constituent materials of composite; matrix and reinforcement. The matrix material surrounds and supports the reinforcement materials by maintaining their relative positions. The reinforcements impart their special mechanical and physical properties to enhance the matrix properties. A synergism produces material properties unavailable from the individual constituent materials, while the wide variety of matrix and strengthening materials allows the designer of the product or structure to choose an optimum combination.

A variety of molding methods can be used according to the end-item design requirements and natures of the chosen matrix and reinforcement materials. Most commercially produced composites use a polymer matrix material often called as a resin solution. There are many different polymers like polyester, vinyl ester, epoxy, phenolic, polyimide, polyamide, polypropylene, PEEK, etc. are available. The reinforcement materials are often in the form of fibers but also commonly ground minerals. The strength of the product is greatly dependent on the percentage of fiber content.

A number of material-processing strategies have been used to improve the wear performance of polymers. This has prompted many researchers to cast the polymers with fibers/fillers. Considerable efforts are being made to extend the range of applications. Various researchers have studied the tribological behavior of FRPCs. Studies have been conducted with various shapes, sizes, types and compositions of fibers in a number of matrices. In general these materials exhibit lower wear and friction when compared to pure polymers. An understanding of the friction and wear mechanisms of FRPC's would promote the development of a new class of materials. [14]

Use of inorganic fillers dispersed in polymeric composites is increasing. Fillers not only reduce the cost of the composites, but also meet performance requirements, which could not have been achieved by using reinforcement and resin ingredients alone. In order to obtain perfect friction and wear properties many researchers modified polymers using different fillers like Al_2O_3, ZnO, CuO, Pb_3O_4, ZrO_2, TiO_2, CuS, MoS_2,

Bronze, Brass, Glass fiber, Carbon, Rubber, Graphite, Oxide Particles, Carbide particles, etc. and even other polymer materials also.[13]

Fiber reinforced polymers or FRPs include wood (comprising cellulose fibers in a lignin and hemicelluloses matrix), carbon-fiber reinforced plastic or CFRP, and glass reinforced plastic or GRP. If classified by matrix then there are thermoplastic composites, short fiber thermoplastics, long fiber thermoplastics or long fiber reinforced thermoplastics. There are numerous thermoset composites, but advanced systems usually incorporate aramid fiber and carbon fiber in an epoxy resin matrix.

Composites can also use metal fibers reinforcing other metals, called as metal matrix composites (MMC). Magnesium is often used in MMCs because it has similar mechanical properties as epoxy. Ceramic matrix composites include bone (hydroxyapatite reinforced with collagen fibers), Cermets (ceramic and metal) and concrete. Ceramic matrix composites are built primarily for toughness, not for strength. Chobham armor is a special composite used in military applications.

The thermoplastic composite materials can also be formulated with specific metal powders resulting in materials with a density range from 2 g/cc to 11 g/cc. These materials can be used in place of traditional materials such as aluminum, stainless steel, brass, bronze, copper, lead, and even tungsten in weighing, balancing, vibration damping, and radiation shielding applications.

Composite materials are popular in high-performance products that need to be lightweight, yet strong enough to take harsh loading conditions such as aerospace components (tails, wings, fuselages, propellers), boat, bicycle frames and racing car bodies. Other uses include fishing rods and storage tanks. The new Boeing787 structure including the wings is composed of over 50 percent composites. Carbon composite is a key material in today's launch vehicles and space crafts. It is widely used in solar panel substrates, antenna reflectors and yokes of space crafts.

PTFE, phenolic, nylon, acetalpolyimide, polysulfone, polyphenylenesulfide,
Ultrahigh molecular weight polyethylene, lubronetc and their composites can be used as bearing materials.

3.2   PTFE and PTFE Composites

Polytetrafluoroethylene (PTFE) resin is a paraffinic thermoplastic polymer that has some or all of the hydrogen replaced by fluoride. It is discovered in 1938 by a DuPont chemist, Mr. Roy J. Plunkett at DuPont's Jackson Laboratory in New Jersey. Upon examination, he learned that PTFE provided a combination of friction, temperature, chemical, mechanical and electrical resisting properties. PTFE is recorded the lowest coefficient of static and dynamic friction as 0.02 - equivalent to wet ice on wet ice. PTFE revolutionized the plastics industry and, in turn, gave birth to limitless applications of benefit to mankind. PTFE is used extensively for a wide variety of structural applications as in aerospace, automotive, earth moving, medical, electrical, electronics, computer and chemical industries.[15]

PTFE has extended chain of linear repeating molecules of CF_2–CF_2. PTFE is a crystalline polymer with a melting point of about 327°C. PTFE has useful mechanical properties from cryogenic temperature of -260°C to higher temperature of 280°C. Pure PTFE has virtually universal chemical resistance, light and weather resistant, resistant against hot water vapor, excellent sliding properties, anti-adhesive behavior, non-combustible, good electric and dielectric properties, no absorption of water, physiologically harmless so as to use in food industry applications. But it has some adverse properties like cold flow behavior, relatively low wear resistance, low resistance to high-energy radiation, poor adhesive behavior and PTFE cannot be injected.[13, 15]

PTFE is a high performance engineering plastics which is widely used in industry due to its properties of self-lubrication, low friction coefficient, high temperature stability and chemically resistant. In fact, PTFE exhibits poor wear and abrasion resistance. To improve the wear resistance suitable fillers are added to PTFE. The most commonly used are glass fiber, carbon, bronze and graphite, in the form of powder intimately mixed with the PTFE, other fillers are molybdenum disulfide, metal powders, ceramics, metal oxides and mixtures of two or more additives.[11]

Molecular structure of PTFE

PTFE is a completely fluorinated polymer manufactured by free radical polymerization of tetrafluoroethylene with a linear molecular structure of repeating –CF_2–CF_2– units.

Molecular structure Polytetrafluoroethylene(PTFE) is a crystalline polymer with a melting point of about 621°F (327°C). PTFE has useful mechanical properties from cryogenic temperatures (-260°C) to 500°F (280°C).

Its coefficient of friction is lower than almost any other material. The chain structure of PTFE has two interesting peculiarities. [15]

3.3   Filler Material

Typical Fillers

a) Glass fiber

PTFE is reinforced with glass fibers, the percentage varying between 5% and 40%. The added glass fiber improves the wear properties to a minor degree, also the deformation strength under load while leaving substantially unchanged the electrical and chemical characteristics.

b) Carbon

Carbon is added to the PTFE in a percentage by weight between 10 and 35%, along with small percentage of graphite. Also, the carbon tends to improve wear & deformation strength .e, while leaving practically unchanged the chemical resistance, but substantially modifying the electrical properties.

c) Bronze

Bronze, when used as filler, is added in percentages of weight between 40% and 60%. Bronze filled PTFE has the best wear properties, remarkable deformation strengths and good thermal conductivity, but poor electrical characteristics and chemical resistance.

d) Graphite

The percentage of graphite varies between 5% and 15%. Graphite lowers the coefficient of friction & is, therefore, often added to other types of filled PTFE for improving this property. It improves the deformation under load, strength &in a minor degree, wears properties.

e) Molybdenum Disulphide

Molybdenum disulfide, minimize friction, furnishes high load performance, reduce power input, prevent metal to metal contact, provide superior protection against wear, adhere well to all types of surfaces, work themselves into surfaces for longer life. [15]

3.4   Manufacturing of PTFE Component

Processing of PTFE is more difficult than that of standard thermoplastics. At high temperatures (340-380°C) PTFE will merely become highly viscous, which means that injection-molding or regular extrusion is impossible. For this reason, semi-finished products are manufactured by means of compression sintering or ram-extrusion. PTFE can be turned, milled, drilled, pierced, broached, ground and polished.

Stages of PTFE Component Manufacturing

a) Resin in Granular Form

PTFE resins are supplied in granular form of uniform density particle and grade. This ensures continuity for all material. This can be done by degradation of PTFE.

b) Extrusion, Molding and Sintering of PTFE

Traditionally, ram or paste extrusion, compression molding or isostatic molding processes PTFE and filled PTFE's. Pressing & Sintering is an extension of these processes and uses powder metallurgy techniques to produce custom sintered PTFE and PTFE filled components.

c) Extrusion

Extrusion is the process where a solid plastic (also called a resin), usually in the form of beads or pellets, is continuously fed to a heated chamber and carried along by a feed screw within. The feed screw is driven via drive/motor and tight speed and torque control is critical to product quality. As it is conveyed it is compressed, melted, and forced out of the chamber at a steady rate through a die. The immediate cooling of the melt results in re-solidification of that plastic into a continually drawn piece whose cross section matches the die pattern desired shape.

d) Compression Molding

Compression molding may be accomplished by either of two methods. The first of these is hydraulic compression molding. In this method, PTFE granules are poured between two metal tubes. A third tube with a slightly smaller outside diameter (O.D.) than the largest tubes inside diameter (I.D.) and a slightly larger I.D. than the smallest tube's O.D. is inserted between the tubes. The assembly is placed in a hydraulic press, where pressure is applied to the middle tube, thus compressing the PTFE.

The other type of compression molding is isostatic compression molding. Isostatic molding is accomplished by compressing PTFE powder between a metal tube and a rubber bladder. The rubber bladder is inflated with very high hydraulic pressure, causing the PTFE powder to be compressed radially. Compression takes place between the I.D. and the O.D. of the billet rather than from the ends (as with hydraulic compression molding). Again, the billet must be sintered to achieve maximum properties.[16]

e) Compression-Sintering

PTFE powder is fed into a cylindrical tool and then condensed under high pressure. An important requirement of this process is that the air contained inside the tool can almost completely escape. The powder is then compressed on speed, pressure and time controlled hydraulic presses. After the compression process, the pre-molded parts are sintered in electrically heated, circulating-air ovens according to specified programs. For optimum compound properties, compression and sintering parameters must be adapted to the respective PTFE compound.

f) Finishing

The molding can now be converted to the finished product by almost any known machine shop technique. PTFE is readily ground and polished to an extremely fine finish, like duroplastics, thermoplastics, elastomers and metals.

3.5   Friction and Wear

3.5.1   Friction

Friction is resistance to motion, which occurs whenever one solid body slides over another. The resistive force, which acts in opposite direction of motion, is known as friction force. The friction force which is required to initiate sliding is known as static friction force, while that required to maintain sliding is known as kinetic friction force. Kinetic friction force is usually lower than static friction force.

The classic laws of friction are as follows:

- Friction force is proportional to load
- Coefficient of friction is independent of apparent contact area.
- Static coefficient is greater than the kinetic coefficient
- Coefficient of friction independent of sliding speed.

The first law, commonly referred as Coulomb's law is correct except at high pressure. It generally takes form

$$F = \mu W.$$

Where,

F = friction force, (N)

μ = coefficient of friction,

W = normal load. (N)

The second law is appears to be valid only for materials possessing a definite yield point (metals), and it does not apply to elastic and viscous elastic materials.

The third law is not obeyed by any viscous elastic material.

The fourth law is not valid for any material, however viscous elastic properties are dominant then this law is obeyed to some extent. [17]

3.5.2 Wear

Wear occurs as natural consequences when two surfaces with a relative motion interact with each other. Wear is a mechanism of removal of material from its surface when it moves to relative to other surface. The mechanism of wear is very complex and is a progressive deterioration of the surfaces with loss of shape often accomplished by loss of weight and creation of debris. It should be note that the real area of contact between two solid surfaces compared with the apparent area of contact is very small, and limited to points of contact between surface asperities. The load applied to the surfaces will be transferred through these points of contact and the localised forces can be very large. Factors governing the wear are material surface properties such as hardness, strength, ductility, work hardening etc. and surface finish, lubrication, load, speed, corrosion, temperature and properties of the opposing surface etc. [15]

Adhesive wear, abrasive wear, liquid erosion, cavitation erosion and fretting wear are the types of material wear.

- **Adhesive Wear**

Adhesive wear is also known as scoring, galling, or seizing. It occurs when two solid surfaces slide over one another under pressure. Surface projections, or asperities, are plastically deformed and eventually welded together by the high local pressure. As sliding continues, these bonds are broken, producing cavities on the surface, projections on another surface, and frequently tiny, abrasive particles, all of which contribute to future wear of surfaces. Therefore adhesive wear is produced by the formation and subsequent shearing of welded junctions between two sliding surfaces. Surfaces which are smooth and held apart by lubricating films, oxide films etc. reduce the tendency of adhesive wear.

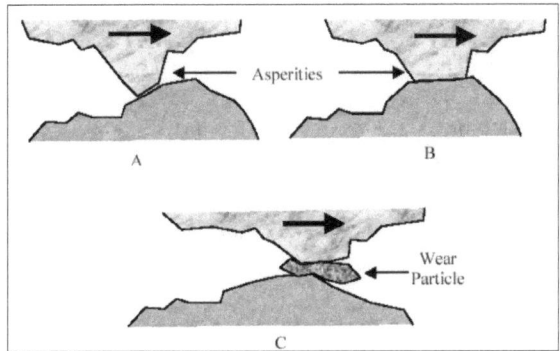

Fig. 3.1 Schematic of adhesive wear process.[2]

- **Abrasive Wear**

Abrasive wear occurs when material is removed by contact with hard particles (either of any surface or loose foreign particle existing between surfaces). The particles either may be present at the surface of a second material (two-body wear) or may exist as loose particles between two surfaces (three-body wear). Two body abrasive wear occurs when one surface (usually harder than the second) cuts material away from the second, although this mechanism very often changes to three body abrasion as the wear debris then acts as an abrasive between the two surfaces. Abrasive wear is common in machineries like scrubber blades, crushers, lapping machines and grinders to remove materials. In dampers, gears, piston and cylinders, abrasive wear occurs.

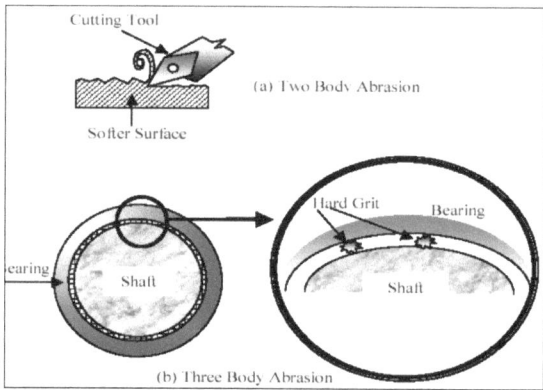

Fig.3.2 Schematic of abrasive wear process.[2]

3.5.3 Liquid Erosion

The integrity of the material may be destroyed by the erosion caused by the high pressure moving liquids may be containing solid particles. The solid particles present in liquid causes the strain hardening of the metal surface leading to localised deformation, cracking and loss of materials.

3.5.4 Cavitation Erosion

Cavitation is the formation and collapse, of cavities or bubbles that contain vapour or gas, within a liquid. Normally, cavitation originates from changes in pressure in the liquid brought about by turbulent flow or by vibration, but can also occur from changes in temperature (boiling). Cavitation erosion occurs when bubbles or cavities collapse on or very near the eroded surface. [15]

18

3.5.5 Fretting Wear

Fretting is a small amplitude oscillatory motion, usually tangential, between two solid surfaces in contact. Fretting wear is the repeated cyclical rubbing between two surfaces, over a period of time which will remove material from one or both surfaces in contact. Fretting wear occurs when repeated loading and unloading causes cyclic stresses which induce surface or subsurface break-up and loss of material. Vibration is a common cause of fretting wear. It occurs typically in bearings, although most bearings have their surfaces hardened to resist the problem. Another problem occurs when cracks in either surface are created, known as fretting fatigue. It is the more serious of the two phenomenons because it can lead to failure of the bearing. An associated problem occurs when the small particles removed by wear are oxidized in air. The oxides are usually harder than the underlying metal, so wear accelerates as the harder particles abrade the metal surfaces further. Fretting corrosion acts in the same way, especially when water is present. Unprotected bearings on large structures like bridges can suffer serious degradation in behavior, especially when salt is used during winter to deice the highways carried by the bridges.

3.6   Properties of PTFE Composite

3.6.1   Physical and Chemical Properties of Unfilled PTFE

The specialty of unfilled PTFE is its combination of superior properties which is unique among plastic compounds

- Exceptionally wide range of thermal applications from $-260°C$ to $300°C$.
- Virtually universal chemical resistance
- Light- and weather-resistant
- Resistant against hot water vapor
- Excellent sliding properties
- Anti-adhesive behavior
- Non-combustible
- Good electric and dielectric properties
- No absorption of water
- Physiologically harmless

3.6.2 Thermal Properties

a) Thermal Resistance

The thermal resistance of PTFE has a range of -260°C to 300°C (i.e. stable in boiling helium at –269°C). No other standard industrial compound can have this temperature range. PTFE may be exposed to temperatures ranging from– 200°C to 260°C.

b) Thermal Expansion

When designing components made of PTFE, the relatively high degree of thermal expansion must be taken into consideration.

c) Thermal conductivity

The coefficient of the thermal conductivity of PTFE does not vary with the temperature. It is relatively high, so that PTFE can be considered to be a good insulating material. The mixing of suitable fillers improves the thermal conductivity.

d) Specific heat

The specific heat, as well as the heat content (enthalpy) increases with the temperature.[32]

3.6.3 Tribological Properties of Bearing Materials

In general, the most important characteristics of bearing materials are

1. **Score Resistance** - A good bearing material should not damage the surface of journal under operating conditions of boundary lubrication. The anti-wear characteristics of bearing material are referred to as a score resistance.

2. **Compressive strength** - This is the ability of the bearing material to carry imposed load without extrusion or disintegration, even if the load without extrusion or disintegration, is variable either in magnitude or direction or both.

3. **Fatigue Strength** - Bearings are usually exposed to fluctuating load, therefore bearing materials should have sufficient fatigue strength.

4. **Deformability** - The bearing material should have an ability to yield and adapt in shape to that of the journal. This property is called conformability. When the journal is deflected under load the contact takes place only at the edges. A confirmable material adjusts its shape under these circumstances. The bearing material should also be able to accommodate any foreign without scoring of journal. This property is called embed ability.

5. **Corrosion Resistance** - Bearing material should resist corrosion due to the lubricant and retain its shape.

6. **Thermal Conductivity** - Running bearings produce heat. This heat can make the lubricant unstable and hence breakage of oils films may happened.. Hence, bearing materials should dissipate heat with higher thermal conductivity.

7. **Thermal Expansion** - Coefficient of thermal expansion should be low for bearing materials to prevent change in size and shape.

8. **Cost and Availability** - The cost of the bearing material should be small in comparison to the total cost of the machine itself. [17]

3.7 Comparison of PTFE+Glass Fiber Material & PTFE + Glass Fiber+MoS$_2$ Material

(1) PTFE + 15%Glass Fiber + 5%MoS$_2$.

(2) PTFE + 15%Glass Fiber.

Property	Unit	PTFE + 15% GF + 5% MoS$_2$	PTFE + 15% GF
Density	g/cm^2	222-225	220-224
Shore Hardness D	Sh.D	54-58	56-64
Tensile Strength (23°c)	N/mm^2	14-18	15-19
Elongation at Break (23°c)	%	200-230	220-260
Tensile Modulus(23°c)	N/mm^2	750	1000
Coefficient of Thermal Expansion(20-100 °c)	1/K.10^{-5}	10-2	10-0
Coefficient of Thermal Expansion(150-260 °c)	1/K.10^{-5}	13-5	13-4
Thermal Conductivity (23°c)	W/K.m	0-35	0-46
Deformation after 24h at 23°c – 15	%	12	12-5
Deformation after 24h at 260°c – 4	%	5	4-8
Compr. Strength at 1% deformation (23°c)	N/mm^2	6-9	8-2
PV-limit 3m/min	N/mm^2.min	25	23
PV-limit 30m/min	N/mm^2.min	28	25
PV-limit 300m/min	N/mm^2.min	32	31
Coefficient of friction – statical		0-15	0-18
Wear K.10^{-8}	cm^3.min/kg .m.h	8-1	7-1

3.8 Area of Applications

With its unusual characteristics, PTFE is a special plastic compound suitable for numerous areas of application:

- Sealing and sliding elements in machinery and automotive manufacturing
- Corrosion protection in chemical industry applications
- Insulating compound for electronics and electrical engineering
- Shrouding and coating of pistons, heating elements, rollers, diaphragms, etc.
- Medical implants as well as medical equipment and componentry
- Food industry
- Tubing/hoses for chemical, pharmaceutical and automotive applications.

Despite higher compound costs, PTFE parts may offer greater cost benefits than conventional volume plastic compounds

PTFE + Glass Fiber + MoS_2 material is preferred in Aircraft application in

- Flight Control
- Helicopter main motor
- Hinges & Linkages

The needs and advantages of accelerated wear testing are discussed, with particular reference to aerospace applications. Examples are given from recent work on plastics-based dry-bearing liners to illustrate how accelerated wear tests can provide information relevant to materials selection, identification of the main parameters influencing wear and definition of the relationships between wear, material composition and structure. Prediction of the service life of dry-bearing liners, however, presents problems and full-scale component tests are usually required. [12]

The operation of aircraft, missiles and satellites embraces almost every conceivable aspect of tribology. A wide range of different types of components is involved together with unequally wide range of materials andtribological processes. Wear problems are many and various, but can broadly be divided in two main groups associated with the diagnosis and rectification of failures and increasing the reliability of components to reduce maintenance and, ultimately, to reduce total life costs. In the early days of aviation, most of the problems encountered fell within the first of the above groups. Component failures were relatively frequent and it was not too difficult to build up a general background of practical experience to aid diagnosis. Tile present position, however, is very different. As aircraft become increasingly sophisticated, improvementsin materials and design are reducing the number of failures and it is no longer always possible to acquire sufficient experience from service. The necessary background must now be provided by the general fund of tribologicalknowledge, supplemented, where necessary, by laboratorytesting. A further consequence of increasing Sophistication in design and construction is that when failures do occur, the consequences can be very expensive.

For example, one bearing failure in the seeking antenna mechanism of a communications satellite can 'write off'' an investment of many millions of pounds. There is also a growing trend towards increasing the service life of aircraft in order to recover as high a proportion as possible of the initial costs. This focuses attention on tile importance of maintenance as a factor in the total 'costs-of-ownership' (production + operation + maintenance); a recent estimate suggests that maintenance an account for up to one-third of the total life costs of a modern, military aircraft .In both of the above groups of problems, basic laboratory studies of wear processes have an important and, arguably, even vital role to play. The purpose of this paper is to identify and describe some of the ways in which such basic studies have proved to be of value. Before doing so, however, it will be useful to discuss briefly a few aspects of the general philosophy of wear testing.

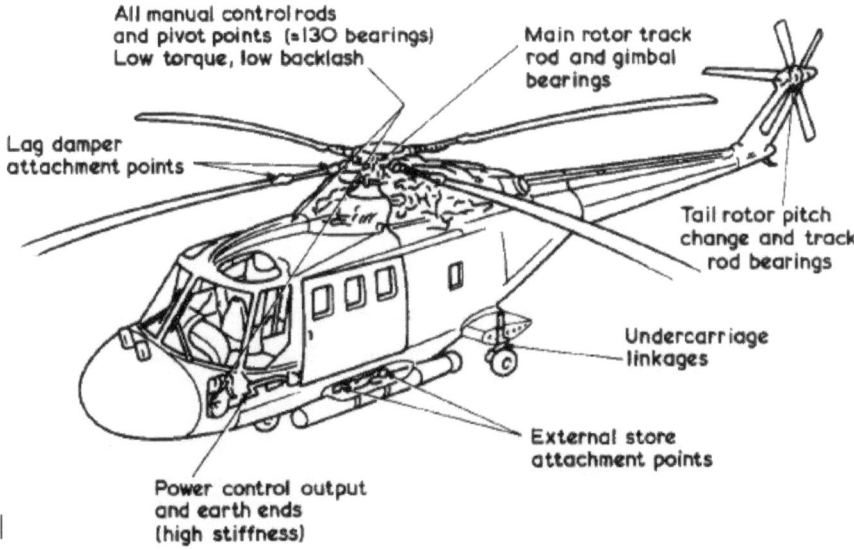

Fig 3.3 Application ofDry Bearing Liners for Flight Control in Helicopter

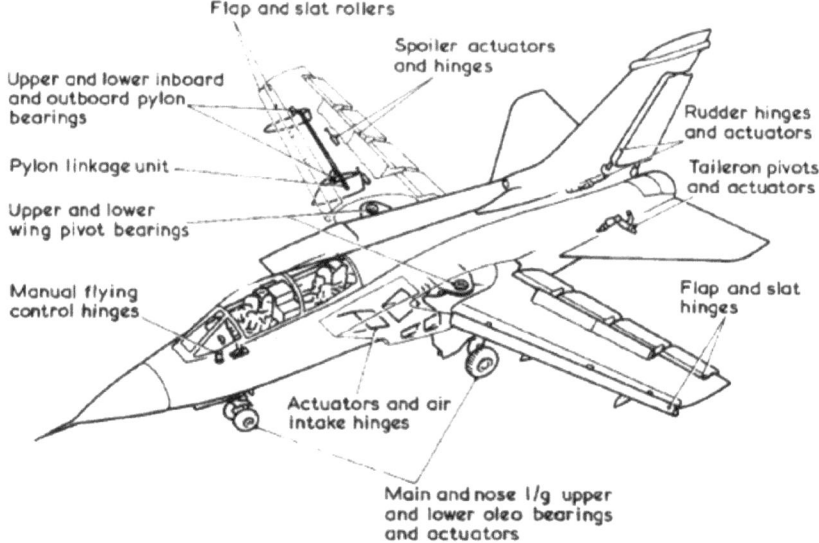

Fig 3.4 Application of Dry Bearing Liners for Flight Control in Fixed Wing Aircraft

One of the most arduous uses of dry bearings for flight-control purposes occurs in helicopters where thin layers of plastics composites containing PTFE are used to permit variations in pitch and position of the rotorblades. The main consequence of wearin these bearings is a gradual increase in 'backlash' which eventually develops to an unacceptable level long before the total thickness of the bearing liners has been worn away. Wear is therefore usually an inconvenience, albeit an expensive one, rather than a disaster. However, exceptions do occur.

In devising any research program which involves measurements of wear, it is critically important to define from the outset exactly what sort of information is being sought because this largely determines the type of test equipment required. Consider as an example, the various possible reasons which exist for testing aircraft flightcontrolbearings used in applications. [12]

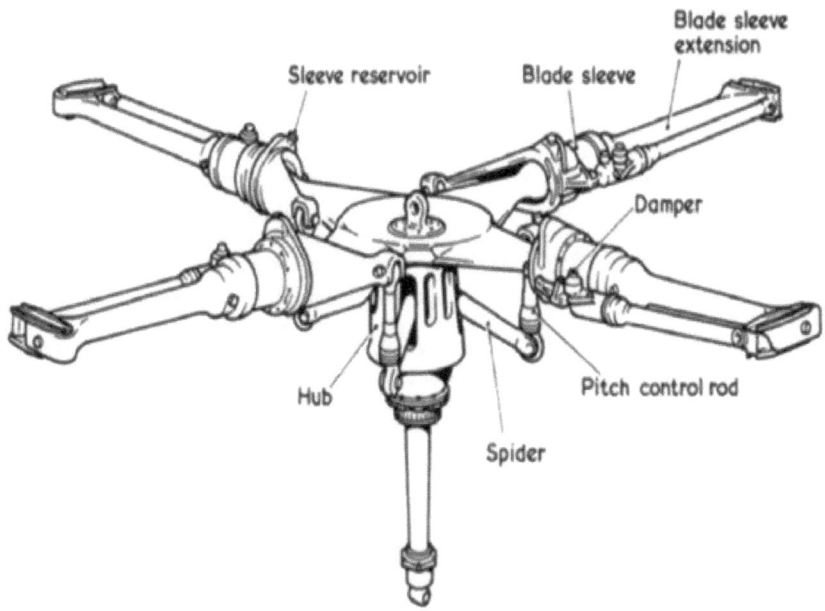

Fig 3.5 Dry Bearing Application in AircraftMain Motor

The materials involved are typically thin liners of plastics composites incorporating PTFE (polytetrafluoroethylene) are used without conventional lubrication by oils or greases. Wear is usuallythe major factor determining 'life-to replacement'. The ideal approach for obtaining the realistic wear-lives of different competitive products is to devise equipment which tests full-scale bearings operating in a spectrum of continuously varying loads, speeds, temperaturesetc.which are characteristic of the typical flight conditions likely to be encountered bya particular aircraft. The data obtained from such tests, however, will be valid only for the conditions imposed andbecause these are complex, extrapolation or interpolation to bearing performance in other areas or in other aircraftis extremely difficult, or even impossible. A more versatile approach is to test bearings at various combinations of constant values of load, speed, temperature etc from which it is then more feasible to extrapolate the data to different bearing applications. This method, however, is even more timeconsuming and expensive than the former. Neither method, moreover, is able to cope with the problem of initial selection of materials, in which bearings from amongst the dozens of different types commercially available are sufficiently promising to be examined in detail. For the latter purposes, a further level of simplification in equipment and procedure is required, indeterminations of wear life in one, constant, arbitrarily-defined set of sliding conditions. Tests of this type frequently form the basis of performance specifications.

Full scale bearings tests are also inappropriate during the early stages of any development program on new materials, where it is important to be able to provide rapid feed-back of performance data to guide further development. An even greater degree of Simplification in wear testing is therefore needed and it is at this stage that apparatus of the pin-on-disc type comes into the picture. The main merit of this sort of equipment is the rapidity with which it is possible to explore the effects of a wide range of changes to material composition and sliding conditions and ultimately to define a general pattern of wear behavior from which performance trends can be predicted. It is important to emphasize that these are only trends because wear data obtained from apparatus of the pin-on-ring type canSeldom be extrapolated directly to predict the life of a bearing in service. Even if most of the service requirements have been carefully simulated, e.g. materials, speed, load and temperature, complicating effects still remain to the shape and size of the sliding specimens. Failure to appreciate this has been responsible for much of the criticism made about the limited practical value of simplified wear testing.[12]

4.   PROBLEM DEFINITION AND OBJECTIVES

4.1   Problem with Friction and Wear

A recent survey showed that the total annual saving that could be made through improved tribological practice can be spilt in following portion

Total annul saving

Reduction in energy consumption from lower friction	5%
Reduction in manpower	2%
Saving in lubricant costs	2%
Saving in maintenance and replacement costs	45%
Saving in losses resulting from breakdown	22%
Saving in investment through greater availability and higher efficiency	4%
Saving in investment through increase life span of plant	20%

Wherever two surface slide, roll or hub against each other, one can be confronted with problem generated by worn surface, problem of high frictional forces, frictional heat or problem of squeak. Polymers offer a wide range of internally lubricated or wear resistant resins that can help to solve these problems.

- **Parts have longer lifetime due to reduced wear**

Excessive wear often leads to premature failure of the part. Higher wear resistant materials allow an increase of time before the need to change a critical part and reduce maintenance costs.

- **Moving system have higher efficiency due to less energy loss through friction**

A low coefficient of friction between two sliding surface reduces the amount of energy that is transformed into heat or noise instead of motion. The motion becomes smoother and more efficient.

- **Sliding surface can bear higher loads and run at higher velocities**

By making the right choice of material, the load bearing capacity higher and sliding speed can be increased, making the system more reliable and powerful.

- **System cost can reduced by elimination any external lubricant**

An efficient internal lubrication of the resin can replace the need for external lubricant and guarantees the right lubrication over the lifetime of the part.

- **Squeaking noise can be reduced below audible limits**

The squeaking noise which did not allow the choice of the same resin for the two sliding surface can now be eliminated by choosing a grade with allow coefficient of friction.

Mechanical properties of PTFE are low as compared to other materials, but its properties remain at a useful level over a wide temperature range of 250 to 295^0C. Mechanical properties are often enhanced by adding filters. It has excellent thermal stability it can withstand temperature up to 294.5^0C and electrical in solution properties and a low coefficient of friction. PTFE is very dense and can't be melt-processed. It must compressed and sintered to form useful shapes.

When Teflon and carbon are formulated and properly blended together, they become an extremely good material for as sea various convenient application. One of the most common additives to assist in blocking ultra-violet light degradation is carbon black. Generally, squeaking of materials that are black in color is UV protected. When left unprotected and exposed to environmental conditions, materials change both in appearance and in their molecular structure. These changes generally manifest themselves in the form of a slight increase in density and a marked decrease in tensile strength values. Thus adding GF and MoS_2 to Teflon we can reduce the effect of the environment. It also improved wear resistance under load and permanent deformation with better thermal and electrical conductivity.

It can handle a very broad range of chemicals with the exception of molten alkali metal and flu. This style is suitable for service at a temperature from the cryogenic range up to 500^0c.This sheet is particularly recommended for application in the industrial and processes industries where high purity material are not required. It is more economical than virgin PTFE and physical properties are not somewhat less than virgin PTFE. Milled glass fibers have the least effect on chemical and electrical properties and add greatly to the mechanical properties of unfilled PTFE.

4.2   Objectives

The purpose of this work is to study the friction and wear behavior of PTFE composites reinforced with adding MoS_2 filler material with glass fiber in PTFE with respect to constantload and sliding velocity, under dry condition at normal temperature and pressure when tested against EN304 stainless steel. It is expected that, this research will be useful in promoting the applications of PTFE composites for constant load and constant speed applications under dry condition.

Following are the objectives of the project work:

1. To find out the behavior of the fabricated material from wear & friction point of view and the effect of constant sliding speed and load on it.

2. To suggest the best suitable self-lubricating PTFE composite material for the Aircraft bearing applications from the tested PTFE composite materials for the existing bearing used for aerospace.

3. To develop relationship between the coefficient of friction, frictional force, velocity and loads.

4. To suggest the best suitable material for the Aircraft bearing applications from the tested materials.

5. To suggest the best suitable surface texture pattern having minimum wear & friction for Aircraft bearing application.

5.   EXPERIMENTATION

To measure the coefficient of friction and wear of two composite materials. One material is PTFE + 15% GF and other material is PTFE + 15% GF + 5% MoS2. Both materials are tested with EN3O4 disc having surface texturing pattern on pin-on disc set-up.

5.1   Apparatus

Pin-on-disc test rig, weights, dial indicator, acetone cotton wastes, cloths etc.

5.2   Experimental Setup

Fig 5.1 Experimental Setup of Tribometer

5.3   Construction

The TR-20LE Pin on disc wear testing is advanced regarding the simplicity and convenience of operation, ease of specimen clamping and accuracy of measurements, bothof wear and frictional force along with lubrication and environmental facility.

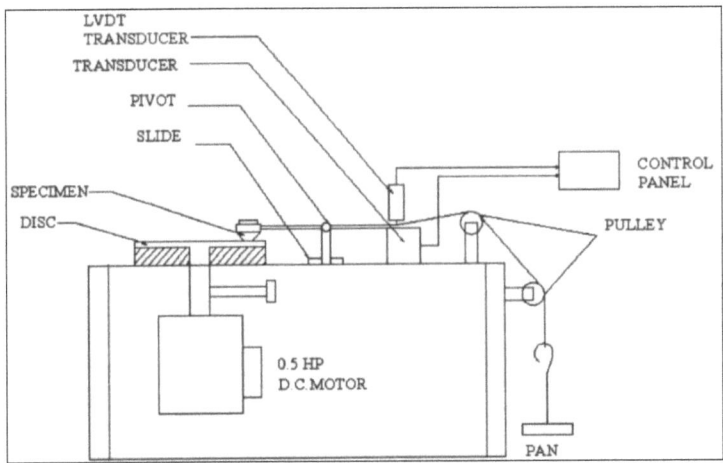

Fig.5.2 Construction of Pin on Disc Apparatus.[2]

The machine is designed to apply loads up to 20 kg and is intended both for dry and lubricated test conditions. It facilitates study of friction andwear characteristics in sliding contacts under desired test conditions within machine specifications. Sliding occurs between the stationary pin and a rotating disc. Normal load, rotational speed and wear track diameter can be varied to suit the test conditions. Tangential frictional force and wear are monitored with electronic sensors and recorded on PC. These parameters are available as a function of load and speed.

The machine consists of spindle assembly, loading lever assembly, sliding plate assembly and environmental chamber, all mounted on base plate over structure made up of welded steel tubes which absorbs entire force and load acting during testing. To minimize the vibration during testing, it is fitted with four numbers of adjustable anti-vibration pads at base. Some items like AC motor, variable frequency drive and all electrical items are fitted inside the structure and sides of it are covered with panels.

The wear disc is mounted on the spindle top and is driven by an AC motor through a timer belt, which provides high torque drive with low vibration. The loading lever with specimen holder fixed at one end and at other end, it carries a wire rope for suspending dead weights to apply normal load on specimen. The frictional force produced between specimen pin and disc is directly measured by the load cell at other end. The specimen pin is placed inside a hardened split jaw and clamped to specimen holder. To clamp different sizes of specimens, individual jaws are provided for different sizes of pin specimens. The oil for test is supplied by a lubrication unit fixed at base of machine.

The wear between specimen pin and disc is measured by LVDT and is sensed by a sensor mounted on lever. The friction between specimen pin and rotating disc is measured by a strain gauge type load cell mounted on a bracket. The spindle speed is measured by proximity sensor through a rpm sensor disc. The machine operation is controlled by a electronic controller which is connected to machine through a set of cables, control cable and signal input cable. The signals passes from machine to controller and then controller processed signals to connected PC. The signals from wear and frictional force sensor are sent to instrumentation card, the output from which is sent to data acquisition card and the output from it is sent to display on controller and to PC. [18]

5.4   Working Procedure

1. Connect the power input cable to 230 V, 50 Hz, and 15 Amps supply. Switch ON controller. Allow 5 minutes for normalizing all electrical items.

2. Using dial indicator, clamp disc within 10 μm run out.

3. Thoroughly clean specimens, remove burs from the circumference using a 2000 grit fine silicon carbide abrasive paper. Clean the wear disc thoroughly with petrol.

4. Insert specimen pin inside the hardened jaws and clamp to specimen holder. Set the height of specimen pin above the wear disc using height adjustment block, ensuring the loading arm always horizontal. Tighten clamping screws on jaws to clamp specimen pin firmly. Swivel off the height adjustment block away from loading arm.

5. Set the required wear track diameter (18 mm to 32 mm) according to sliding speed by moving the sliding plate over graduated scale on base plate. Tighten both the clamping screws to ensure assembly is clamped firmly.

6. Wear display: Loosen LVDT lock screw, rotate thumbscrew to bring LVDT plunger visually to mid position, the wear reading display on controller should be as near to zero. Initialize wear display to '0' by pressing 'ZERO' push button on controller.

7. Frictional force display: Move loading arm away from frictional force load cell and set frictional force display '0' by pressing relative 'ZERO' button on controller.

8. Place required weights on loading pan to apply constant normal load.

9. Setting disc speed: Set 10 minute time on controller, press test, start push button and rotate. Set by rotating rpm knob on controller till required test speed is displayed. Continually run for the remaining time to observe any fluctuation. Press STOP button.

10. Setting test duration on controller: Test duration is set either in time mode (set in hr, min, sec) or counter mode (set in no. of cycles, max. is 100000 cycles). Mode

selection is by the toggle switch below timer display, the switch position indicates selection as either time or counter. Test duration of 60 minutes is selected.

11. Setting of computer for testing and data acquisition:

- Connect the data acquisition cable from controller to PC.
- Open the software Winducom 2008 on PC.
- Click on mode run continuously icon on software screen to activate screen.
- Click on ACQUIRE tool bar at screen top to open acquiring screen.
- Enter a name on file name window.
- In the cell for Sample ID, enter the material of the specimen and its dimensions.
- Fill the remaining empty cells for speed, load, wear track and data sampling rate.
- In the Remark cell, enter dry test, duration of test, speed etc.
- Click START button in PC window.
- Press START push button on the controller front panel to commence the test and send data to PC.
- Set the required rpm by rotating slowly the rpm knob in clockwise direction.
- Measured rpm is displayed on the SPEED window of the controller front panel. .
- Click zero button on PC screen and initialize all sensor values to zero.
- Click SAVE button on PC screen to save data

On controller the acquired test parameters like wear, frictional force, speed and temperature are displayed, the same values are displayed on PC screen with graph.

Specifications of PIN and Disc Tribometer (TR-20LE)

- Overall Size   660 × 630 × 860 mm.(L × b × h)
- Pin Size   3,4,6,8, 10 and 12 mm diameter.
- Disc Size   165 mm diameter × 8 mm thick
- Wear Track Diameter (Mean)   15 mm to 100 mm.
- Loading Lever Length   394 mm.
- Sliding Speed Range   0.05 m/sec. to 10 m/sec.
- Disc Rotation Speed   20-2000 RPM with LC 1 rpm.
- Normal Load   5 N to 200 N.
- Friction Force   0 to 200 N, digital recorded output
- Wear Measurement Range   ± 2 mm LC 0.1 μm digital recorded output.
- Power   1.5 kW, 230 V, 15A, 1 Phase, 50 Hz

5.5   Materials and Test Conditions

5.5.1   Variables in Wear Testing

The variables in Wear Testing are as follows.

a)Normal Load

In this experiment for the application of aerospace the load is constant as 12kg that is 117.75N is to taken for the experimentation.

b) Sliding Velocity

Table 5.1 Running parameters selected for experimental analysis.

Sr.No.	Load(N)	Velocity(m/s)	Time(min)
1.0	12	0.12	60

c) Temperature

In this 3particular experimental work no such facilities were available for the test rig. So the readings are taken at the room temperature.

d) Contact Area

Contact area between the pin and disc is28.27 mm². (Pin dia. is 6 mm.)

e) Sliding Time

Sliding time is kept 60 minutes for all mating surfaces.

f) Surface finish

Surface finish of the EN3O4 stainless steel disc is measured by surface tester and its average value is $R_a = 0.14$ μm. While during experimentation wearing surface of the test pins are polished with the help of 2000 grit fine silicon carbide abrasive paper so as too obtained high surface finish.

f) Material

Counterface-1 is nothing but the pin material. It was changed according to the different pins used as listed in table 5.2 and table 5.3

Table 5.2 Material composition of experimental samples of PTFE composites

Sample	Matrix	Filler Particles	%weight	Condition
A	PTFE	Glass Fiber	15	Filler
B	PTFE	Glass Fiber + MoS_2	15+5	Filler

Twenty test pins of each material samples are prepared so as to take the test for each normal load and sliding velocity.

Table 5.3 Material composition of EN3O4stainless steel disc.

Content	C	Si	Mn	P	S	Cr	Ni
Percentage	0.08	0.75	2.00	0.045	0.03	18	10

g) Lubricant

No lubricant was used during the test conditions.

5.6   Measured Parameters

a) Friction Measurements

The lever transmits a signal through a load cell for determining frictional force. Load cell is connected to digital panel, which displays the frictional force and also connected to PC where it is recorded. The readings are recorded manually for every 5 minutes of interval.

b) Wear Measurement

Electronic LVDT wear measurement is used for permanently recording wear. The readings are recorded manually for every 5 minutes of interval.

c) Test Time

Digital timer/controller for automatic shut off.

d) Cycle Counter

Panel mounted cycle counter gives the RPM of the rotating disc.

5.7   Calculation

The Speed of Rotation of Disc.

With the help of dimple track diameters & constant sliding velocity.

We know that,

Sliding velocity, V = 0.12 m/s

1) For First Dimple Track,

   Minimum Diameter = 12 mm

   Maximum Diameter = 24 mm

So, Mean Diameter = 18 mm

There for, mean radius, r = 9 mm

Now, We know that,

   $V = r*\omega$

Where,

V = Sliding velocity, (m/s)

r = mean radius of dimple track, (m)

ω = angular velocity of disc, (rad/s)

Now, $\omega = V/r$

$\omega = 0.12/0.009$

$\omega = 13.3334$ rad/s

But, $\omega = 2*\Pi*N/60$

Where,

N = rotation speed of disc (rpm)

Now, $13.3334 = 2*\pi*N/60$

N = 127.3245 rpm

2) Similarly, for second dimple track,

N = 71.6197 rpm

3) Similarly, for third dimple track,

N = 49.8224 rpm

5.8   Pin Specimen Material

Table 5.4 Material composition of experimental samples of PTFE composites with quantities

Specimen Material	Quantity
PTFE+15%Glass Fiber	10
PTFE+15%Glass Fiber +5%MoS$_2$	10

5.9 Observations

Table No. 5.5 Observation table for plane surface of Material-A

Material: PTFE + 15% GF   Condition: Dry   Speed: 39rpm

Weight: 12kg   Pin Dia.: 6mm   Plane Surface

Sr.No.	Time(min)	Wear(μ)	Frictional Force(N)	COF
1	0	0	56.8	0.482
2	5	0	57.6	0.489
3	10	0	58.1	0.493
4	15	0	59.4	0.504
5	20	0	61.9	0.525
6	25	0	58.9	0.5
7	30	0	59.0	0.501
8	35	1	58.3	0.495
9	40	2	58.4	0.496
10	45	2	58.5	0.496
11	50	3	60.4	0.513
12	55	3	60.5	0.513
13	60	3	60.1	0.51

Table No.5.6 Observation table for track-2 of Material-A

Material: PTFE+15% GF   Condition: Dry   Speed: 127rpm

Weight: 12kg   Pin Dia.:6mm   Size: 100 μ & 10%

Sr.No.	Time(min)	Wear(μ)	Frictional Force(N)	COF
1	0	0	40.9	0.347
2	5	0	48.4	0.411
3	10	1	49.6	0.421
4	15	2	48.1	0.408
5	20	2	48.1	0.408
6	25	3	48.3	0.41
7	30	3	48.1	0.408
8	35	3	47.9	0.406
9	40	3	47.6	0.404
10	45	3	48.1	0.408
11	50	2	48.3	0.41
12	55	3	47.9	0.406
13	60	3	48.3	0.41

Table No. 5.7 Observation table for track-3 of Material-A

Material: PTFE + 15% GF   Condition: Dry   Speed: 72rpm

Weight: 12kg   Pin Dia.: 6 mm   Size: 200µ & 10%

Sr.No.	Time(min)	Wear(µ)	Frictional Force(N)	COF
1	0	0	25.5	0.2166
2	5	0	27.3	0.2319
3	10	0	28.8	0.2446
4	15	1	28.4	0.2412
5	20	1	28.9	0.2454
6	25	1	29.8	0.2531
7	30	1	30.6	0.259
8	35	2	32.4	0.275
9	40	1	34.6	0.293
10	45	1	36.5	0.31
11	50	2	36.5	0.31
12	55	2	40.5	0.344
13	60	2	42.5	0.361

Table No. 5.8 Observation table for track-4 of Material-A

Material: PTFE + 15% GF   Condition: Dry   Speed: 51rpm

Weight: 12kg   Pin Dia.: 6mm   Size: 300µ & 10%

Sr.No.	Time(min)	Wear(µ)	Frictional Force(N)	COF
1	0	0	46.5	0.395
2	5	0	58.6	0.497
3	10	1	58.7	0.498
4	15	1	56.1	0.476
5	20	1	58.4	0.496
6	25	1	58.3	0.495
7	30	1	57.8	0.49
8	35	2	57.8	0.49
9	40	2	58.9	0.5
10	45	2	58.3	0.495
11	50	3	59.2	0.502
12	55	3	57.6	0.489
13	60	3	55.8	0.474

Table No. 5.9 Observation table for track-5 of Material-A

Material: PTFE+ 15% GF   Condition: Dry   Speed: 127rpm

Weight: 12kg   Pin Dia.: 6mm   Size: 100μ& 20%

Sr.No.	Time(min)	Wear(μ)	Frictional Force(N)	COF
1	0	0	30	0.254
2	5	0	32.4	0.275
3	10	0	41.4	0.351
4	15	0	44.4	0.377
5	20	1	45	0.382
6	25	1	45.1	0.383
7	30	1	45.1	0.383
8	35	1	45.4	0.385
9	40	2	45.4	0.385
10	45	2	45.5	0.386
11	50	2	46.2	0.392
12	55	2	46.8	0.397
13	60	2	47	0.399

Table No. 5.10 Observation table for track-6 of Material-A

Material: PTFE+ 15% GF   Condition: Dry   Speed: 72rpm

Weight: 12kg   Pin Dia.:6mm   Size: 200μ & 20%

Sr.No.	Time(min)	Wear(μ)	Frictional Force(N)	COF
1	0	0	29.6	0.251
2	5	0	34.4	0.292
3	10	1	39.8	0.338
4	15	1	45.5	0.386
5	20	2	47.1	0.400
6	25	3	48.8	0.414
7	30	4	49.3	0.418
8	35	5	49.8	0.423
9	40	5	50.2	0.426
10	45	5	50.6	0.429
11	50	5	51.1	0.434
12	55	6	50.3	0.427
13	60	6	50.4	0.428

Table No. 5.11 Observation table for track-7 of Material-A

Material: PTFE + 15% GF   Condition: Dry   Speed: 51rpm

Weight: 12kg   Pin Dia.: 6mm   Size: 300µ & 20%

Sr.No.	Time(min)	Wear(µ)	Frictional Force(N)	COF
1	0	0	27.5	0.233
2	5	1	27.7	0.235
3	10	1	32.1	0.272
4	15	2	37.1	0.315
5	20	2	38.8	0.329
6	25	3	41.2	0.349
7	30	4	40.8	0.346
8	35	4	40.0	0.339
9	40	5	42.4	0.36
10	45	6	42.8	0.363
11	50	6	43.3	0.367
12	55	7	43.5	0.369
13	60	8	44.0	0.373

Table No. 5.12 Observation table for track-8 of Material-A

Material: PTFE + 15% GF   Condition: Dry   Speed: 127rpm

Weight: 12kg   Pin Dia.: 6 mm   Size: 100µ & 30%

Sr.No.	Time(min)	Wear(µ)	Frictional Force(N)	COF
1	0	0	32.4	0.275
2	5	0	33.8	0.287
3	10	0	42.3	0.359
4	15	0	46.2	0.392
5	20	0	48	0.407
6	25	0	48.3	0.41
7	30	0	49.1	0.417
8	35	1	50	0.424
9	40	1	50.3	0.427
10	45	1	50.5	0.428
11	50	1	50.7	0.43
12	55	1	50.3	0.427
13	60	1	49.8	0.423

Table No. 5.13 Observation table for track-9 of Material-A

Material: PTFE+ 15% GF   Condition: Dry   Speed: 72 rpm

Weight: 12kg   Pin Dia.:6mm   Size: 200µ& 30%

Sr.No.	Time(min)	Wear(µ)	Frictional Force(N)	COF
1	0	0	38.9	0.33
2	5	0	43.6	0.37
3	10	0	46.8	0.397
4	15	0	48.8	0.414
5	20	0	49	0.416
6	25	1	49.1	0.417
7	30	1	48.8	0.414
8	35	1	48.9	0.415
9	40	2	48.9	0.415
10	45	1	48.9	0.415
11	50	2	48.2	0.409
12	55	2	47.9	0.406
13	60	2	48.0	0.407

Table No. 5.14 Observation table for track-10 of Material-A

Material: PTFE+ 15% GF   Condition: Dry   Speed: 51rpm

Weight: 12kg   Pin Dia.: 6mm Size: 300µ& 30%

Sr.No.	Time(min)	Wear(µ)	Frictional Force(N)	COF
1	0	0	33.4	0.283
2	5	0	51.2	0.434
3	10	0	52.1	0.442
4	15	0	53.3	0.452
5	20	1	54.7	0.464
6	25	1	55.1	0.468
7	30	1	55	0.467
8	35	1	55.2	0.468
9	40	2	55.4	0.47
10	45	2	54.9	0.466
11	50	2	54.8	0.465
12	55	3	54.4	0.462
13	60	3	53.8	0.457

Table No. 5.15 Observation table for plane surface of Material-B

Material: PTFE + 15% GF + 5% MoS$_2$ Condition: Dry   Speed: 39rpm

Weight: 12kg   Pin Dia.: 6mm   Plane Surface

Sr.No.	Time(min)	Wear(μ)	Frictional Force(N)	COF
1	0	0	50.5	0.428
2	5	0	63.3	0.537
3	10	0	66.8	0.567
4	15	0	69.7	0.592
5	20	0	69.3	0.588
6	25	0	68.9	0.585
7	30	1	69.9	0.5937
8	35	1	69.7	0.5920
9	40	1	70.2	0.5963
10	45	2	70.3	0.5971
11	50	2	70.2	0.5963
12	55	2	71.4	0.6065
13	60	2	71.5	0.6073

Table No. 5.16 Observation table for track-2 of Material-B

Material: PTFE + 15% GF + 5%MoS$_2$ Condition: Dry   Speed: 127rpm

Weight: 12kg   Pin Dia.: 6mm   Size: 100μ & 10%

Sr.No.	Time(min)	Wear(μ)	Frictional Force(N)	COF
1	0	0	36.2	0.307
2	5	0	47.6	0.404
3	10	0	47.7	0.405
4	15	1	47.5	0.403
5	20	1	46.8	0.397
6	25	1	46.2	0.392
7	30	1	46.1	0.391
8	35	1	46.3	0.393
9	40	1	46.6	0.395
10	45	1	47.2	0.4
11	50	1	48.1	0.408
12	55	1	48.6	0.412
13	60	1	48.8	0.414

Table No. 5.17 Observation table for track-3 of Material-B

Material: PTFE+ 15% GF + 5% MoS$_2$ Condition: Dry   Speed: 72rpm

Weight: 12kg   Pin Dia.:6mm   Size: 200µ & 10%

Sr.No.	Time(min)	Wear(µ)	Frictional Force(N)	COF
1	0	0	26.5	0.2251
2	5	0	43.4	0.3686
3	10	1	45.3	0.3848
4	15	1	45.6	0.3873
5	20	1	45.8	0.3890
6	25	1	46.1	0.3916
7	30	2	46.6	0.3958
8	35	2	47	0.3992
9	40	2	46.4	0.3941
10	45	2	46.6	0.3958
11	50	2	47.2	0.4009
12	55	2	47.5	0.4034
13	60	2	47.8	0.4060

Table No. 5.18 Observation table for track-4 of Material-B

Material: PTFE + 15% GF + 5% MoS$_2$ Condition: Dry   Speed: 51rpm

Weight: 12kg   Pin Dia.: 6mm   Size: 300 µ & 10%

Sr.No.	Time(min)	Wear(µ)	Frictional Force(N)	COF
1	0	0	39.8	0.3380
2	5	0	48.5	0.4119
3	10	1	49.5	0.4204
4	15	1	50.5	0.429
5	20	1	51.3	0.435
6	25	1	51.5	0.437
7	30	1	51.2	0.434
8	35	2	50.9	0.432
9	40	2	50.7	0.43
10	45	2	52.3	0.444
11	50	2	53.2	0.451
12	55	3	53.5	0.454
13	60	3	53.5	0.454

Table No. 5.19 Observation table for track-5 of Material-B

Material: PTFE+ 15% GF + 5% MoS$_2$ Condition: Dry   Speed: 127rpm

Weight:12kg   Pin Dia.: 6mm   Size: 100 μ& 20%

Sr.No.	Time(min)	Wear(μ)	Frictional Force(N)	COF
1	0	0	28.2	0.239
2	5	0	32.0	0.271
3	10	0	38.2	0.324
4	15	1	40.6	0.344
5	20	1	40.7	0.345
6	25	1	41.3	0.35
7	30	1	41.8	0.355
8	35	1	42.9	0.364
9	40	1	43.5	0.369
10	45	1	43.7	0.371
11	50	1	43.5	0.369
12	55	1	43.6	0.37
13	60	1	43.6	0.37

Table No. 5.20 Observation table for track-6 of Material-B

Material: PTFE + 15% GF + 5%MoS$_2$ Condition: Dry   Speed: 72rpm

Weight: 12kg   Pin Dia.: 6mm   Size: 200 μ & 20%

Sr.No.	Time(min)	Wear(μ)	Frictional Force(N)	COF
1	0	0	29.9	0.2539
2	5	0	43.6	0.3703
3	10	1	46.5	0.3950
4	15	1	46	0.3907
5	20	1	46.2	0.3924
6	25	1	46.2	0.3924
7	30	1	45.5	0.3865
8	35	1	46.5	0.3950
9	40	1	46.2	0.3924
10	45	1	46.6	0.3958
11	50	2	46.8	0.3975
12	55	2	47.2	0.4009
13	60	2	47.5	0.4034

Table No. 5.21 Observation table for track-7 of Material-B

Material: PTFE+ 15% GF + 5% MoS$_2$ Condition: Dry   Speed: 51rpm

Weight: 12kg   Pin Dia.: 6mm   Size: 300 μ & 20%

Sr.No.	Time(min)	Wear(μ)	Frictional Force(N)	COF
1	0	0	28.1	0.238
2	5	0	40.4	0.343
3	10	1	45.5	0.386
4	15	1	46.8	0.397
5	20	1	46.8	0.397
6	25	3	45.5	0.386
7	30	2	45.8	0.389
8	35	2	44.8	0.38
9	40	2	45.5	0.386
10	45	3	45.0	0.382
11	50	2	44.4	0.377
12	55	2	45.0	0.382
13	60	2	45.6	0.387

Table No. 5.22 Observation table for track-8 of Material-B

Material: PTFE+ 15% GF + 5% MoS$_2$ Condition: Dry   Speed: 127rpm

Weight: 12kg   Pin Dia.: 6mm   Size: 100 μ& 30%

Sr.No.	Time(min)	Wear(μ)	Frictional Force(N)	COF
1	0	0	26.8	0.227
2	5	0	27.4	0.232
3	10	0	31.9	0.27
4	15	0	34.0	0.288
5	20	1	35.9	0.304
6	25	1	37	0.314
7	30	1	37.5	0.318
8	35	1	37.7	0.32
9	40	1	37.9	0.321
10	45	1	38.0	0.322
11	50	1	38.2	0.324
12	55	1	38.4	0.326
13	60	1	38.5	0.327

Table No. 5.23 Observation table for track-9 of Material-B

Material: PTFE+ 15% GF + 5% MoS_2 Condition: Dry   Speed: 72rpm

Weight: 12kg   Pin Dia.: 6mm   Size: 200 μ& 30%

Sr.No.	Time(min)	Wear(μ)	Frictional Force(N)	COF
1	0	0	26.7	0.226
2	5	0	46.6	0.395
3	10	1	48.6	0.412
4	15	1	48.9	0.415
5	20	2	48.8	0.414
6	25	2	49.1	0.417
7	30	2	49.4	0.419
8	35	2	49.7	0.422
9	40	2	49.8	0.423
10	45	2	49.7	0.422
11	50	2	49.5	0.42
12	55	2	49.6	0.421
13	60	2	49.3	0.418

Table No. 5.24 Observation table for track-10 of Material-B

Material: PTFE+ 15% GF + 5% MoS_2 Condition: Dry   Speed: 51rpm

Weight: 12kg   Pin Dia.: 6mm   Size: 300 μ&30%

Sr.No.	Time(min)	Wear(μ)	Frictional Force(N)	COF
1	0	0	40.2	0.341
2	5	0	45.1	0.383
3	10	0	47.6	0.404
4	15	0	48.8	0.414
5	20	0	47.9	0.406
6	25	0	49.1	0.417
7	30	0	49.1	0.417
8	35	0	50.4	0.428
9	40	0	50.6	0.429
10	45	0	50.4	0.428
11	50	0	50.2	0.426
12	55	1	50.2	0.426
13	60	1	50.0	0.424

5.10   Calculations

5.10.1 Sample calculations for Material (A)

Material = PTFE + 15% GF   Size = 10% & 100μ

$$K = W/ (PVt)$$

Where,

      K = Specific wear rate (mm^3/Nm)

      W = Volumetric losses (mm^3)

      P = Load (N)

      V = Sliding velocity (m/s)

      t = Time (sec)

But, the sliding velocity is,

$$V = (2*\pi*N*D)/60$$

Where,

      V = velocity (m/s)

      N = Speed (rpm)

      D = radial distance (mm)

So,

$$V = (2*3.14*127*30*10^{-3})/60$$

$$V = 0.39898 \text{ m/s}$$

Now, Specific Wear Rate is

$$K = (\pi/4*6^2*2*10^{-3}) / (12*9.81*0.39898*3600)$$

$$K = 3.3444*10^{-7} \text{ mm}^3/Nm$$

Then, the coefficient of friction,

$$F = \mu W$$

Where,

      F = friction force (N)

      μ = coefficient of friction

      W = normal load (N)

So,

$$\mu = (48.3/12*9.81)$$

$$\mu = 0.4102$$

5.10.2 Sample calculations for Material (B)

Material= PTFE + 15% GF + 5% MoS$_2$ Size = 10% & 100 μ

$$K = W/ (PVt)$$

Where,

      K = Specific wear rate (mm^3/Nm)

      W = Volumetric losses (mm^3)

      P = Load (N)

      V = Sliding velocity (m/s)

      t = Time (sec)

But, the sliding velocity is,

$$V = (2*\pi*N*D)/60$$

Where,

      V = velocity (m/s)

      N = Speed (rpm)

      D = radial distance (mm)

So,

      V=(2*3.14*127*30*10^{-3})/60

      V= 0.39898 m/s

Now, Specific Wear Rate is

      K=(π/4*6^2*1*10^{-3})/(12*9.81*0.39898*3600)

      K=1.6722*10^{-7} mm^3/Nm

Then, the coefficient of friction,

F= μW

Where,

      F = friction force (N)

      μ = coefficient of friction

      W = normal load (N)

So,

      μ= (48.8/12*9.81)

      μ = 0.4145

5.11 Results

Table No.5.25 Result Table for PTFE+ 15% Glass Fiber

Sr. No.	Size (μ & density)		Speed (rpm)	Wear (μ)	Sliding Velocity (m/s)	Wear rate (mm³/Nm)	Coefficient of friction
1	100μ	10%	127	2	0.39898	$3.344*10^{-7}$	0.4048
2		20%		2		$3.344*10^{-7}$	0.3683
3		30%		1		$1.6722*10^{-7}$	0.3931
4	200μ	10%	72	2	0.22619	$5.8992*10^{-7}$	0.3801
5		20%		6		$1.7697*10^{-7}$	0.3900
6		30%		2		$5.8992*10^{-7}$	0.4022
7	300μ	10%	51	3	0.16022	$1.2492*10^{-7}$	0.4848
8		20%		8		$3.3312*10^{-7}$	0.3275
9		30%		3		$1.2492*10^{-7}$	0.4464

Table No.5.26 Result table for PTFE + 15% Glass Fiber+5%MoS₂

Sr. No.	Size (μ & density)		Speed (rpm)	Wear (μ)	Sliding Velocity (m/s)	Wear rate (mm³/Nm)	Coefficient of friction
1	100μ	10%	127	1	0.39898	$1.6722*10^{-7}$	0.3944
2		20%		1		$1.6722*10^{-7}$	0.3421
3		30%		1		$1.6722*10^{-7}$	0.3
4	200μ	10%	72	2	0.22619	$5.8992*10^{-7}$	0.2722
5		20%		2		$5.8992*10^{-7}$	0.4122
6		30%		2		$5.8992*10^{-7}$	0.4
7	300μ	10%	51	3	0.16022	$1.2492*10^{-7}$	0.4386
8		20%		2		$8.3282*10^{-7}$	0.3717
9		30%		1		$4.1641*10^{-7}$	0.4114

5.12 Graphs

Material (A) - PTFE + 15 % Glass Fiber

Material (B) – PTFE + 15 % Glass Fiber + 5 % MoS_2

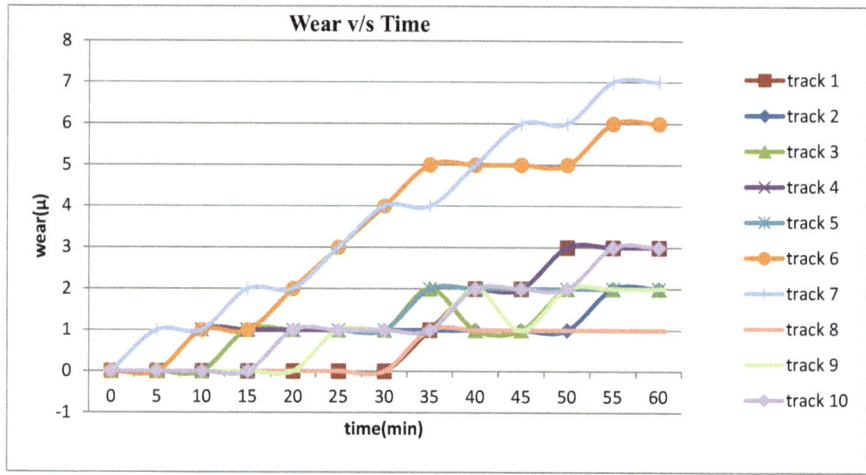

Graph No.5.1 Wear v/s Time for PTFE + 15% Glass Fiber (Material-A)

From above graph we observed that dimple size in μ increases then wear also increases. From track- 2, 3 & 4 consist of same density 10% and changing dimple size in μ, we observe that track-4 having more wear than track-2 & 3 which consist of 10% density & 300 μ size.

Dimple density in % increases then weardecreases.From track- 2, 5 & 8 consist of same dimple size in μ but changing the density, we observe that track-8 having less wear than track-2 & 5 which consist of 30% density & 100 μ size.

So, Track-8 (Material- PTFE + 15% GF, size-100 μ & 30% density) having less wear. Track-7 (Material- PTFE + 15% GF, size- 300 μ & 20% density) having high wear.

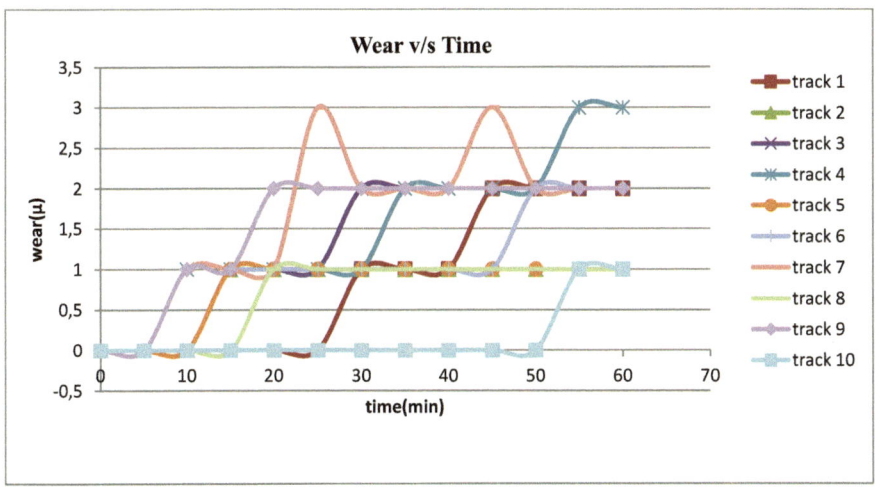

Graph No. 5.2 Wear v/s Time for PTFE + 15% GF + 5% MoS$_2$ (Material-B)

From above graph we observed that dimple size in μ decreases then wear also decreases. From track- 5, 6 & 7 consist of same density 20% and changing dimple size in μ, we observe that track-5 having less wear than track-6 & 7 which consist of 20% density & 100 μ size.

Dimple density in % increases then weardecreases.From track- 4, 7 & 10 consist of same dimple size in μ but changing the density, we observe that track-10 having less wear than track-4 & 7 which consist of 30% density & 300 μ size.

So, Track-8 (Material- PTFE + 15% GF, size-100 μ & 30% density) having less wear. Track-7 (Material- PTFE + 15% GF, size- 300 μ & 20% density) having high wear.

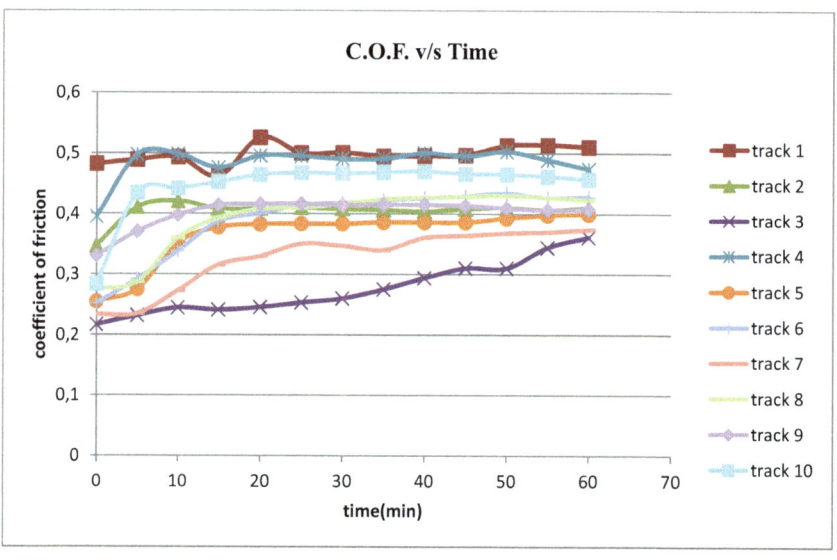

Graph No. 5.3 C.O.F. v/s Time for PTFE + 15% GF (Material-A)

From above graph we observed that dimple size in μ increases then C.O.F. also increases. From track- 8, 9 & 10 consist of same density 30% and changing dimple size in μ, weobserve that track-10 having more C.O.F. than track-8 & 9 which consist of 30% density & 300 μ size.

Dimple density in % increases then C.O.F. decreases. From track- 3, 6 & 9 consist of same dimple size in μ but changing the density, we observe that track-9 having less C.O.F. than track-3 & 6 which consist of 30% density & 200 μ size.

Track-1 (Material- PTFE + 15% GF, Plane surface) having high coefficient of friction.On plane surface, the coefficient of friction is higher than the texturing surfaces. Track-3 (Material- PTFE + 15% GF, size- 200 μ & 10% density) having less C.O.F. So from this observed that by addition of surface texturing friction decreases.

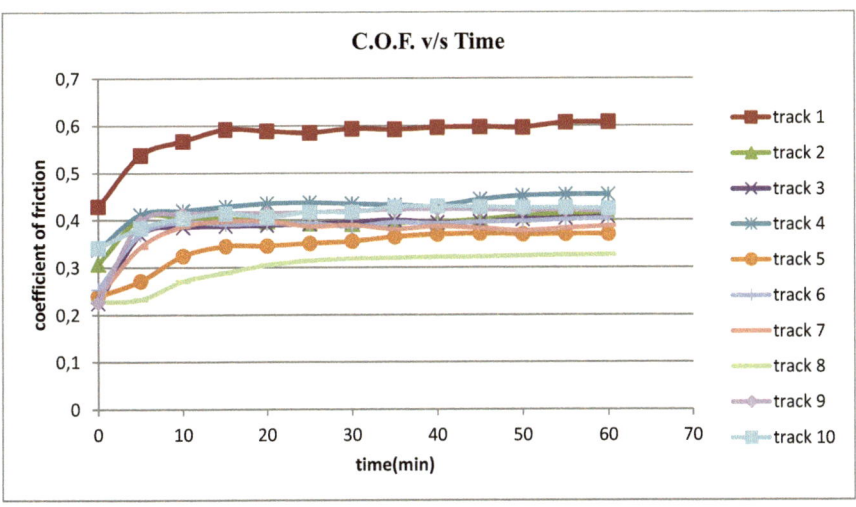

Graph No. 5.4 C.O.F. v/s Time for PTFE + 15% GF + 5% MoS$_2$(Material-B)

From above graph we observed that dimple size in µ increases then C.O.F. also increases. From track- 5, 6 & 7 consist of same density 20% and changing dimple size in µ, we observe that track-7 having more C.O.F. than track-5 & 6 which consist of 20% density & 300 µ size.

Dimple density in % increases then C.O.F. decreases. From track- 2, 5 & 8 consist of same dimple size in µ but changing the density, we observe that track-8 having less C.O.F. than track-2 & 5 which consist of 30% density & 100 µ size.

Track-1 (Material- PTFE + 15% GF, Plane surface) having high coefficient of friction.On plane surface, the coefficient of friction is higher than the texturing surfaces. Track-8 (Material- PTFE + 15% GF + 5% MoS$_2$, size- 100 µ & 30% density) having less C.O.F.So from this observed that by addition of surface texturing friction decreases.

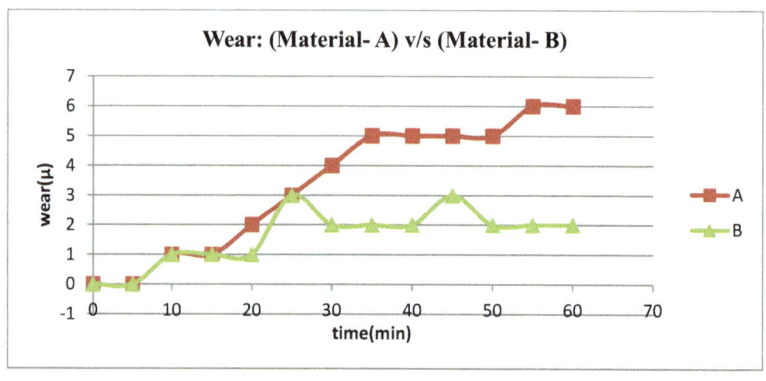

5.5 Graph of Comparison of wear between two materials

The optimum graphs of both materials are drawn and observe the wear.

The Material PTFE + 15% GF + 5% MoS$_2$ having less wear than the Material PTFE + 15% GF.

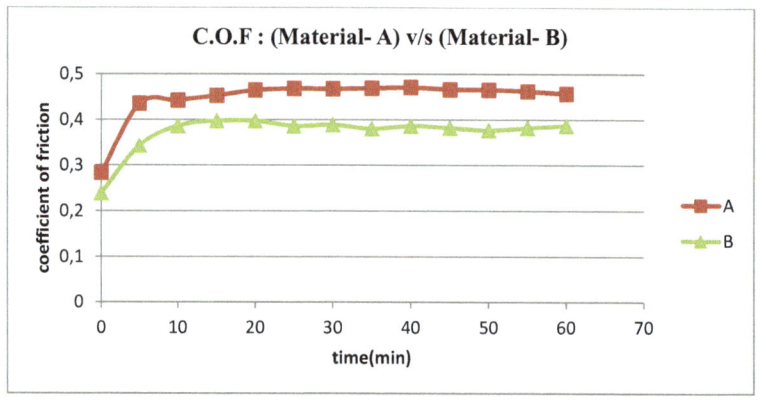

5.6 Graph of comparison of COF between two materials

The optimum graph of both materials are drawn and observe the C.O.F.

The Material PTFE + 15% GF + 5% MoS$_2$ having less C.O.F. than the Material PTFE + 15% GF.

6. CONCLUSIONS AND FUTURE SCOPE

6.1 Conclusions

- The material PTFE + 15% GF + 5% MoS_2 having less wear & less coefficient of friction than the material PTFE + 15% GF.
- The C.O.F. & wear on plane surface is higher than the textured surface.
- As dimple size in μ increases then wear & C.O.F. also increases.
- As density of the dimples increases then the wear & C.O.F. decreases.
- Material-B (PTFE + 15% GF + 5% MoS_2) is good in wear resistant and friction resistant than the Material-A(PTFE + 15% GF).
- Glass fibers with the presence of a small amount of MoS_2 particulates (5%) in PTFE cause a significant increase in the wear resistance.
- Wear resistance of PTFE +15% Glass Fiber +5% MoS_2 shows better results as compared to PTFE+ 15% Glass Fiber so it can be suggested as the suitable material for Aircraft bearings application .

6.2 Future Scope

There are many variables that could be taken in wear testing such as load, velocity, temperature, contact area, surface finish, sliding distance, environment, counter face material, type of lubricant, hardness of counter face etc. In this present experimental investigation, variables like contact area, temperature, test duration (sliding distance), hardness of counter surface and load were kept constant. But it can be varied to get wear rate of PTFE Composite for the change in these variables.

- Analogous to this experimentation, tests could be done for more percentage of solid lubricants like MoS_2 and graphite.
- Scanning Electronic Microscopy photographic analysis of the counter surface could be carried out and more conclusions about the present investigations could be drawn in favor of wear mechanism.
- The test could be done for varying load, surface finish, sliding velocity.
- The test could be conducted by considering effect variables like temperature, and humidity on the friction and wear behavior of PTFE composites.

REFERENCES

1. Jaydeep Khedkar, IoanNegulescu, Efstathios I. Meletis(2002) "Sliding wear behavior of PTFE composites "Elsevier.com"

2. Junxiang Wang etc all.(2003) Investigation of the influence of MoS_2 filler on the tribological properties of carbon fiber reinforced nylon 1010 composites "Elsevier.com"

3. Jaydeep Khedkar etc. all(2002) Sliding wear behavior of PTFE composites"Elsevier.com"

4. A Shalwan etc. all (2013) In State of Art: Mechanical and tribological behaviour of polymeric composites based on natural fibres"Elsevier.com"

5. Jun hong jia Etc. all (2005) Comparative investigation on the wear and transfer behaviors of carbon fiber reinforced polymer composites under dry sliding and water lubrication"Elsevier.com"